Series consultant and author: Brian Williams
Educational consultant: Daphne Ingrams

Illustrators: Vincent Wakerley
(cover and pages 20-21, 24-25, 28-31, 36-37, 42-43,
50-51, 84-85, 88-89)
Oxford Illustrators (pages 14-17, 22-23,
26-27, 34-35, 38-41, 44-49, 54-59,
73, 98-99, 102-119)
Andrew French (pages 66-67, 70-71, 74-75)
David McAllister (pages 82-83, 86-87, 90-91, 92–93 *top*)
Peter Dennis (pages 12-13, 52-53, 96-97)
Tony Gibbons and Lawrie Taylor (pages 64-65,
68-69, 72, 80-81, 92-93 *bottom*, 100-101)
Graham White (pages 60-61)
Industrial Art (pages 78-79)

Designer: Robert Wheeler
Editor: Sian Hardy

First American edition, 1993

YOUNG WORLD is a trademark of Random House, Inc.

Library of Congress Cataloging in Publication Data
Williams, Brian.
  On the move / by Brian Williams.
  —1st American ed.
    p.   cm.—(Young world; 4)
Includes index.
  Summary: Introduces different kinds of
transportation by land, air, sea, and space.
  1. Transportation—Juvenile literature.
[1. Transportation.] I. Title. II. Series: Young world
(New York, N.Y.)
TA149.W55   1993
629.04—dc20   92–21678
            ISBN 0–679–83694–2
        ISBN 0–679–93694–7 (lib.bdg.)

Manufactured in Spain
1 2 3 4 5 6 7 8 9 10

YOUNG WORLD

On the
Move

Random House 🏠 **New York**

About YOUNG WORLD

For every young child, the world is full of new discoveries, new knowledge. It is important to have information books that enable even the youngest to enjoy making these discoveries and gathering this knowledge for themselves.

YOUNG WORLD introduces a wide range of the topics that absorb children. The books in this series are all carefully prepared by specialist authors with the help of experienced educational advisers and teachers so that information is presented simply and memorably. Each book is complete in itself, yet builds into a multi-volume set—a real encyclopedia for the vital first years at school.

Because YOUNG WORLD books are small and easy to handle, children can dip into them on their own or read them with the help of a parent or a teacher. On every eye-catching page, a great deal of thought has been put into matching the clear, readable text with beautiful illustrations. These books are designed to encourage children to find facts for themselves, opening the door to a world where discovering and learning are fun.

About this book

Whenever you catch a bus, ride in a car, or pedal a bicycle, you are using a form of transportation.

Transportation means carrying things and people from place to place. Early forms of transportation were slow. Today, journeys that used to take days, or even weeks, take only a few hours. A jet airplane can fly around the world in just one and a half days.

Because transportation has become faster, easier, and cheaper, our world and the way we live have changed. Our cities have airports. Roads, tunnels, and bridges crisscross the countryside. People often travel to faraway places, and our stores are filled with goods from all over the world. We depend on transportation.

People around the world travel in many different ways. In some countries people drive on the right-hand side of the road. In others they drive on the left. In this book we have shown a mixture of left- and right-hand driving, as well as a selection of license plates from different countries.

Brian Williams, author

CONTENTS

WHEELS ON RAILS

OCEAN
TRANSPORTATION

 INTO THE AIR

THE SPACE AGE

All kinds of

transportation

✸ A busy street

This busy street is full of people on the move. A truck delivers fish that has come from far away to a store. A bus takes people to work or school. All around us are cars, trucks, and motorcycles carrying people and things from one place to another.

✸ Around the world

Much of the food we eat every day comes from faraway places. Have you ever thought how it reaches us?

Roads and railroads join cities that are hundreds of miles apart. Big container ships bring us food from countries across the sea.

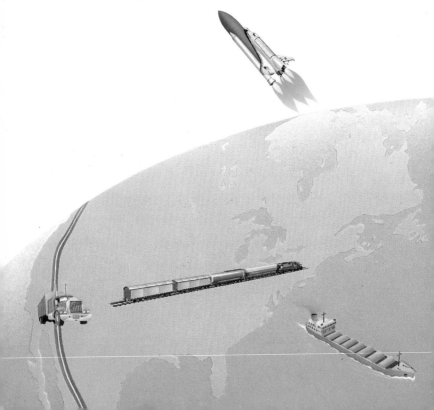

Planes travel faster than ships or trains or trucks. A big jet can fly around the world in only one and a half days. Some planes carry cargo, but most are used to carry passengers. Rockets can now even carry people into space.

✱ Animal power

People cannot always use cars and trains to move around. In some places it would be too difficult to build a road or a railroad.

Camels can walk for days across a hot desert. Most cars would sink into the sand. In the jungle, the easiest way to get around is often to take a canoe down the river.

When this happens, people often use animals to help them carry their heavy loads from place to place.

High up in the mountains of Peru, people use llamas to carry their loads. In Lapland, the Lapps use reindeer to pull their sleds across the snowy ground.

Amazing facts

✺ The wheel was the first important transportation invention. People first made wheels over 5,000 years ago. They made them by fastening pieces of wood together.

✺ The world's longest highway system is the Pan American Highway. It is nearly 17,000 miles long, although there is a gap in the middle. It starts in Alaska in the far north of North America and ends in Brazil in South America.

✺ The biggest parking lot in the world is in Edmonton, in Canada. It has parking spaces for 30,000 cars.

Wheeling

along

🏍 A bicycle

On a bicycle you use your feet to move the pedals. Follow the numbers to find out what happens next.

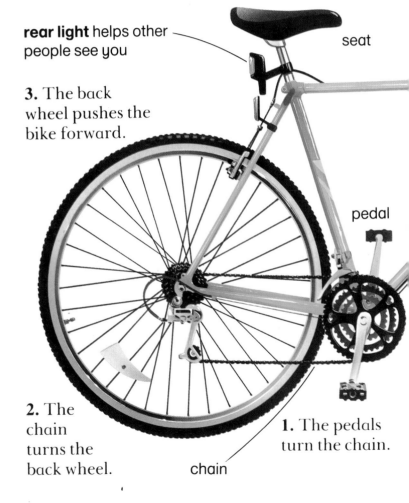

rear light helps other people see you

seat

3. The back wheel pushes the bike forward.

pedal

2. The chain turns the back wheel.

1. The pedals turn the chain.

chain

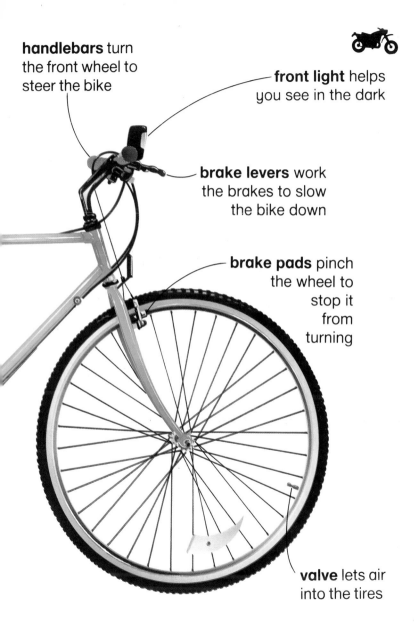

handlebars turn
the front wheel to
steer the bike

front light helps
you see in the dark

brake levers work
the brakes to slow
the bike down

brake pads pinch
the wheel to
stop it
from
turning

valve lets air
into the tires

21

🏍 Bicycle safety

Riding a bike is fun, but always remember: safety first! Check your bike regularly and take it to a repair shop if anything is wrong. Learn the highway laws before riding your bike on the road. The picture below shows you eight things you need for your bike.

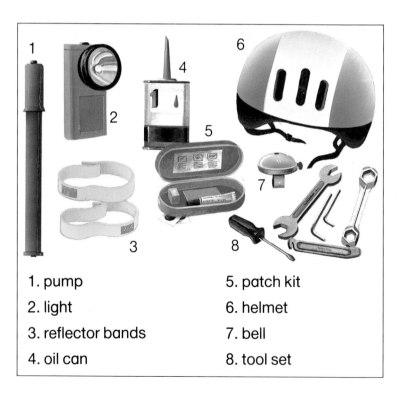

1. pump	5. patch kit
2. light	6. helmet
3. reflector bands	7. bell
4. oil can	8. tool set

Make sure the brake pads have not worn
down and always keep your chain well oiled.

You may need help to fix
a flat tire. First find
the hole in the inner
tube, and then cover
it with a patch.

Early bikes

People have enjoyed riding on two wheels ever since the bicycle was invented.

The hobbyhorse was an early bike with no pedals. You pushed yourself along with your feet.

Later bikes, like the velocipede, had pedals fixed to the front wheel.

Because of its big front wheel, the high-wheeler could go very fast. But it was difficult to ride.

24

🏍️ One, two, three wheels

A one-wheeled cycle is called a unicycle, and a three-wheeled cycle is called a tricycle.

Could you balance on a unicycle?

This racing tandem bicycle is built for two people. The front rider steers the bike.

In some Asian cities, pedal-powered rickshaws are used as taxis.

🏍 A motorcycle

A motorcycle is powered by a gasoline engine. The engine drives a shaft or a chain that turns the back wheel. The back wheel pushes the motorcycle forward.

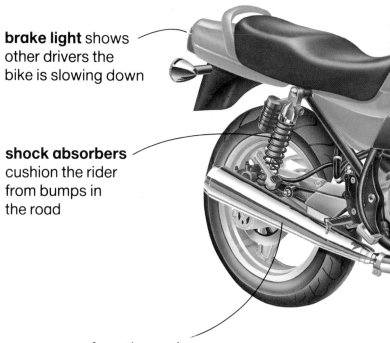

brake light shows other drivers the bike is slowing down

shock absorbers cushion the rider from bumps in the road

waste gases from the engine escape through the **tail pipe**

mirror

speedometer shows how
fast the bike is going

brake lever

tank holds gasoline to
fuel the engine

headlight

turn signal

gasoline engine

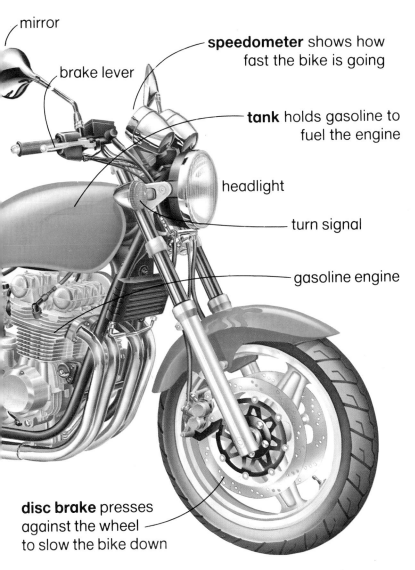

disc brake presses
against the wheel
to slow the bike down

27

🏍 Working bikes

The police use fast motorcycles. Unlike
cars, which need lots more space,
motorcycles are not held up in traffic jams.
So a police motorcyclist can quickly reach
an accident and call for help by radio.

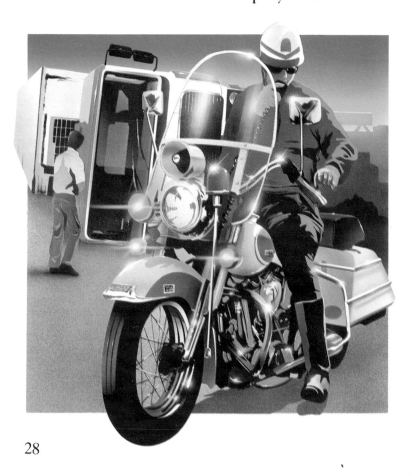

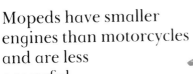 # All kinds of bikes

Mopeds have smaller
engines than motorcycles
and are less
powerful.

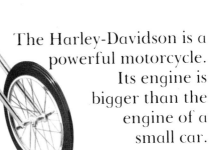

The Harley-Davidson is a
powerful motorcycle.
Its engine is
bigger than the
engine of a
small car.

A sidecar fixed to the
side of a motorcycle
can carry an extra
passenger.

 Racing bikes

People enjoy racing bikes and motorcycles.
They race on tracks and on roads. Racers
use bikes that are faster than ordinary
bikes.

The Tour de France
is the most famous
bicycle race.
The race is in
stages and lasts
about three weeks.

In motocross races, riders scramble over bumps and through streams on their motorcycles.

Drag bikes only race along a short track, but they reach speeds of over 185 miles an hour in a few seconds.

Grand Prix racers speed around a winding track. The riders lean into the curves to keep their balance.

Amazing facts

Air-filled bicycle tires were invented by John Dunlop about 60 years after the first bicycle appeared. Before that, bicycle wheels had metal or wooden rims. This made them very uncomfortable to ride.

The Tour de France is the longest bicycle road race. It covers more than 1,800 miles, but is broken into stages.

The fastest speed on a motorcycle is over 318 miles an hour. This record was set by Donald A. Vesco in 1978 on a bike with two engines.

A "wheelie" means riding on the back wheel only. The record for a wheelie on a motorcycle is an amazing 205 miles nonstop.

Four wheels

more wheels

33

 A car

A car has hundreds of parts. It has a strong metal frame, called a chassis, and a body made of thin metal panels. Follow the numbers to see how it works.

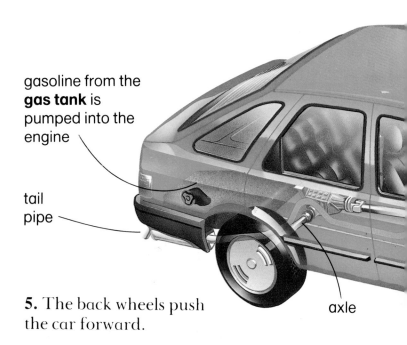

gasoline from the **gas tank** is pumped into the engine

tail pipe

axle

5. The back wheels push the car forward.

In some cars the engine turns the front wheels. This is called front-wheel drive.

4. The drive shaft turns the axle, and this turns the back wheels.

1. Turning the key starts the engine.

2. Gasoline in the engine is mixed with air. Electric sparks make the mixture explode over and over again, pushing pistons up and down.

windshield

battery

radiator helps cool the engine

drive shaft

engine

3. The pistons turn the drive shaft.

front disc brakes

Big cars, small cars

Cars come in many shapes and sizes. People use them for all kinds of different jobs.

This car has big wheels for driving across rough ground.

Cars with powerful engines can tow heavy loads.

A sports car has a long, low shape. This helps it go fast.

A station wagon has lots of room to store luggage in.
A luggage rack can be useful too.

Taxis carry people
around towns
and cities.

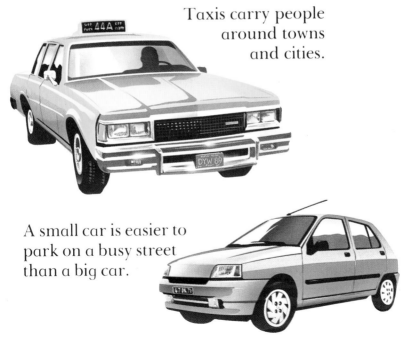

A small car is easier to
park on a busy street
than a big car.

Driving then and now

When cars were first invented, driving was a real adventure. The cars often broke down, and there were no good roads. People wore coats to stay warm and goggles to keep dust out of their eyes.

Driving is very different today. Modern cars are fast and comfortable, and roads and highways crisscross the country. But there are so many cars that they cause traffic jams and pollute the air with their exhaust.

At the garage

Like all machines, cars need care.

Without gasoline the car will not go. The oil in the engine should be checked regularly. The air pressure in the tires should also be checked from time to time. Keeping a car clean helps protect it against rust.

At the garage, mechanics service and repair cars. They check the engine, brakes, and other parts and replace them if they have worn out. They can raise the car on a lift to work underneath it.

![truck icon] Racing cars

Racing cars are built to go much faster than ordinary cars. During a race, they can reach speeds of nearly 250 miles an hour. Air rushing over the airfoils at the front and back of the car pushes the car downward to help keep the wheels on the track.

If the weather is dry, racing cars use tires called slicks. Slicks have no tread, or pattern, cut in them. If the track is wet, treaded tires are used – they give a better grip on the track.

 Buses

The first buses were pulled by horses. Later there were buses on rails, called streetcars. Today most buses have diesel engines.

This brightly colored bus is used in Pakistan. When the bus is full, people sit on the roof.

This London double-decker bus can carry more than 70 people.

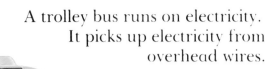

A trolley bus runs on electricity.
It picks up electricity from
overhead wires.

An articulated bus is
extra long. The bus
can bend at the joint
to go around corners.

Some buses take people
on long-distance
journeys.

A tractor-trailer

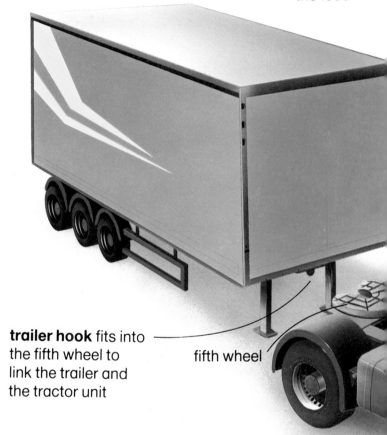

trailer carries the load

trailer hook fits into the fifth wheel to link the trailer and the tractor unit

fifth wheel

diesel fuel for the engine is carried in the **fuel tank**

A tractor-trailer is made up of two parts: a trailer and a tractor. The trailer is like a big container. It has no engine and is pulled along by the tractor. Because a tractor-trailer is made up of two parts, it can go around tight corners.

wind deflector pushes air out of the truck's way

mirror

tractor pulls the trailer

lights

47

The truck driver

At a busy warehouse, a forklift operator
loads the trailer. Once everything is in
place, the driver can set off. On a long trip,
he may be away from home for a week or
more.

A truck driver uses a CB (citizens band) radio to keep in touch with other drivers. A jack comes in handy if he has to change a tire. After a hard day's driving, he climbs into his bunk bed at the back of the cab. At the end of the journey, he hands over his delivery papers and the trailer is unloaded.

Special trucks

Trucks are designed and built for the different jobs they do.

A tanker carries gasoline or chemicals inside a strong metal tank.

The trailer of a refrigerator truck is cold inside, like a refrigerator or freezer, to keep food fresh.

A car carrier transports new cars from the factory to the showroom.

This logging truck has a crane to lift logs onto the trailer.

A roadtrain is a truck that pulls three or more trailers. It is used on very long journeys.

Emergency!

Fire! Cars and bike riders make way for the emergency vehicles as they speed through the streets. Firefighters are soon at work putting out the fire. Police officers keep people away from the danger area. The ambulance arrives in case anyone is hurt.

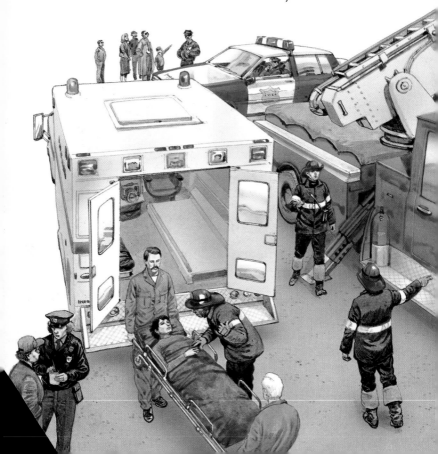

▄▄▄ Off the road

The farm tractor has a powerful engine and big back wheels. The deep tread, or pattern, on the tires helps them grip the mud when the tractor is pulling a heavy plow up and down a field.

The big tires on this all-terrain vehicle help it travel over rough ground. It can climb steep hills and splash through mud and water. To steer, the driver uses handlebars instead of a steering wheel.

A mobile crane

The mobile crane can travel on roads like any truck. But at the building site, it puts down metal legs, called stabilizers, that raise it off the ground and keep it steady as it lifts its heavy load.

Pulley wheels wind the load up and down on wires.

The driver pulls levers inside the cab to work the crane's arm, or boom.

stabilizers

The boom can be made longer or shorter, like a telescope.

boom

57

🚛 Building a road

First, planners make maps to show where the new road will go. They work out how much traffic will use the road. Then, huge machines get to work building the road.

1. Bulldozers clear away piles of rocks and earth.

2. Machines called scrapers level the ground to make it flat.

dump truck

3. Dump trucks carry away the waste soil and deliver a mixture of crushed stones. This is pressed into the earth to make a firm base for the road. Graders then smooth the surface of the road so it is ready for the top layer.

steamroller

4. A paving machine spreads a layer of asphalt on the road. Finally, a steamroller presses the asphalt down to make it smooth and hard.

bulldozer

scraper

grader

paving
machine

59

🚛 Bridges and tunnels

Bridges and tunnels shorten journeys.
A bridge can carry railroad tracks across a
river, or take cars safely over another road.
Tunnels allow us to go through mountains,
beneath city streets, and under rivers.

To build a tunnel, engineers must bore through rock under the ground. If the rock is hard, machines drill holes for explosives that will blast the rock away.

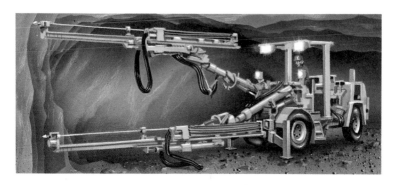

If the rock is softer, a tunnel-boring machine is used. This has a cutting face that bites away the rock. The tunnel is then lined with steel and concrete.

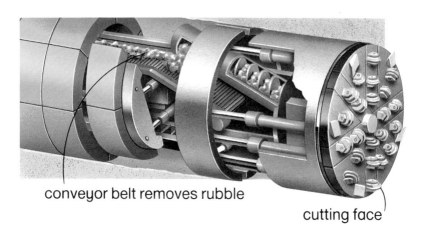

conveyor belt removes rubble

cutting face

Amazing facts

There are more than 500 million cars in the world. About one third of them are driven in North America.

The biggest land vehicles are two giant crawlers used to carry space rockets to the launch pad at Cape Canaveral in Florida. Each is as big as a twelve-story building.

The world's fastest passenger car is the Jaguar XJ220. It can go over 200 miles an hour.

The fastest land vehicle in the world is *Thrust 2*. This car has jet engines and can travel at over 630 miles an hour.

The Saint Gotthard Tunnel is the world's longest road tunnel. It is over 10 miles long and burrows beneath the Alps in Switzerland.

Wheels

on rails

🚂 At the station

Trains start and end their journeys at stations. Stations are busy places, with people hurrying to catch their trains. Schedule boards show passengers which platform to go to and what time the train will depart.

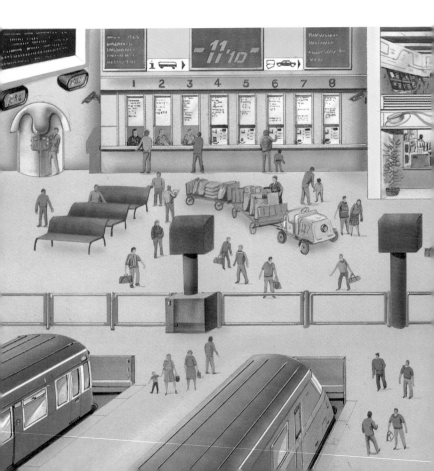

Trains come and go all day long. A fast express train may be taking passengers to a city hundreds of miles away. Slower trains bring people to work in the city. Trains carry letters and packages too.

🚂 A high-speed train

This French TGV is the world's quickest passenger train. (In French, TGV stands for "high-speed train".) The TGV travels at speeds of up to 200 miles an hour. Its streamlined shape helps it to go fast.

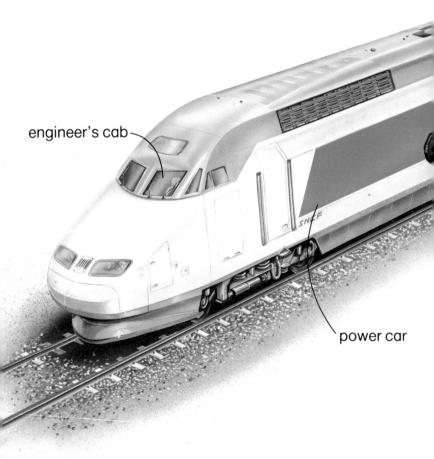

engineer's cab

power car

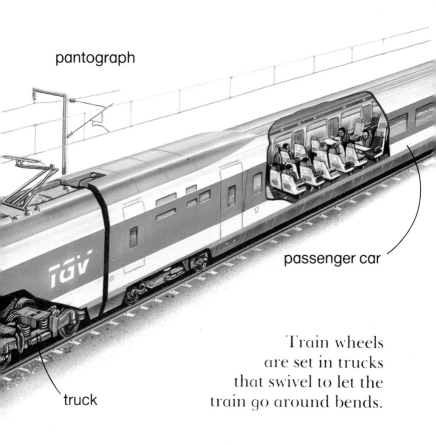

pantograph

passenger car

truck

Train wheels
are set in trucks
that swivel to let the
train go around bends.

The TGV is powered by electricity. It picks
up electricity from an overhead wire with a
sliding arm called a pantograph. Motors in
the power cars use this electricity to drive
the wheels and pull the train along.

67

🚂 Driving a train

Inside the engineer's cab on a TGV there is a computer that tells the engineer how fast he can go and when to slow down and stop. The engineer controls the speed of the train with the wheel in front of him.

Train wheels have no tires. Instead they have a rim, or flange, on the wheel's inner edge to stop them from slipping off the rail. Movable tracks, called switches, shift the train from one track to another. The switches are controlled electronically from a control room far away.

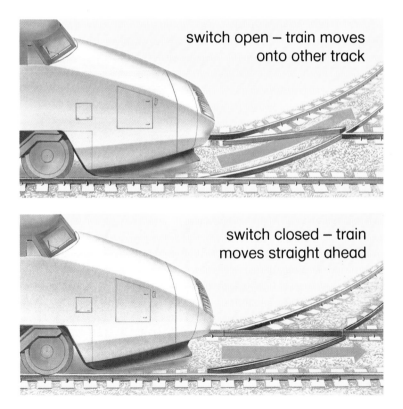

switch open – train moves onto other track

switch closed – train moves straight ahead

A steam train

A steam train burns wood or coal to heat water and make steam. The steam then pushes pistons that turn the wheels.

This steam train traveled across North America over 100 years ago. The cowcatcher in front cleared the track.

Trains around the world

Steam trains are still used on some railroads. This one is in India.

A modern diesel-electric train burns oil to make electricity. The electricity drives the train's motors.

A cog railway is designed to climb steep hills. It has an extra wheel with teeth that fit into notches on a third rail. This stops the train from slipping down the hill.

third rail

🚂 Underground

Subway trains carry people through tunnels under busy city streets. The trains run on electricity. Passengers go down in elevators or on escalators or stairs.

Overground

Like a train that runs underground, a hanging monorail can save space in a busy city. "Monorail" means the train travels on just one rail. A hanging monorail, such as the one shown above, hangs below the rail. A sturdy arm holds it in place. Other monorails sit on the rail.

Freight trains

As well as carrying passengers, trains also transport all kinds of goods, called freight, from one place to another.

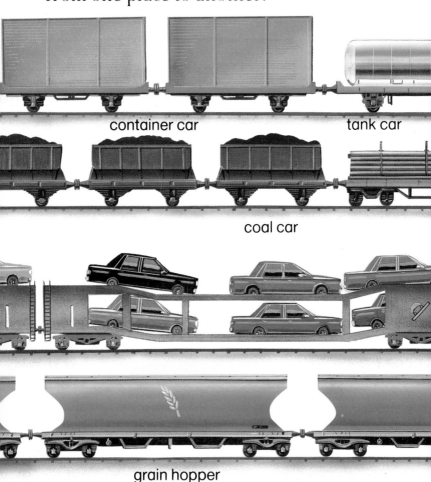

container car

tank car

coal car

grain hopper

Freight trains can be made up of as many as 150 different cars. They are linked together in a freight yard.

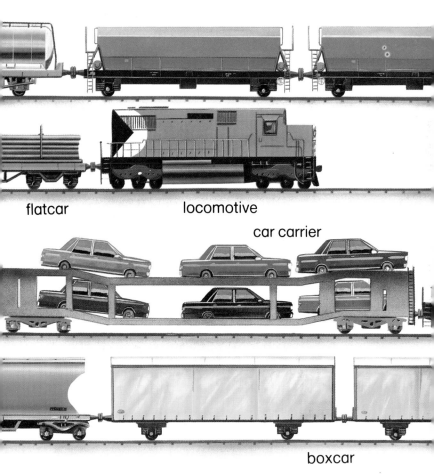

flatcar

locomotive

car carrier

boxcar

Amazing facts

The first public steam railroad was the Stockton and Darlington Railway, in England. In 1825 a train made up of 33 cars carried the first passengers at a top speed of 15 miles an hour.

The first underground railroad opened in London in 1863. The trains were pulled by steam locomotives, and the tunnels were always full of smoke.

The speed record for a train is 320 miles an hour. This was set by a French TGV in 1990. New trains that are being developed, called Maglev trains, could go even faster. Maglev trains float above the track and are pushed along by magnets.

The longest railroad line in the world is over 5,800 miles long and runs from Moscow to Nakhodka, in Russia.

Ocean

transportation

A port

At a port, ships are loaded and unloaded. Tugboats guide big ships to their docking places, called berths. Huge cranes lift cargo off the ships to be stored in warehouses. To keep the water deep, dredges scoop up mud from the bottom.

ferry

warehouse

dredge

tugboat

crane

An ocean liner

An ocean liner is like a floating hotel. The passengers enjoy their journey in comfort. They can swim, play games on deck, or watch a film while the crew runs the ship.

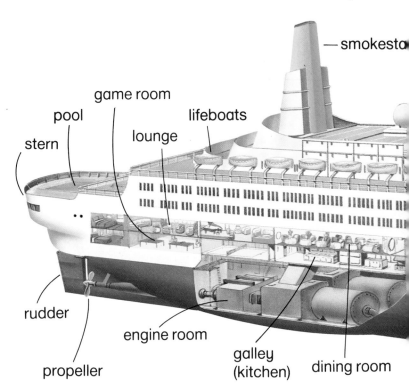

smokestack

game room

pool

lifeboats

stern

lounge

rudder

engine room

galley (kitchen)

dining room

propeller

The parts of a ship all have names. The body is called the hull. The front is called the bow, and the back is called the stern. Bedrooms are called cabins, and the kitchen is called the galley. The captain controls the ship from the bridge.

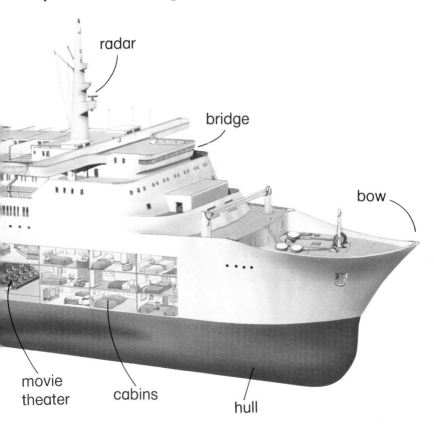

radar

bridge

bow

movie theater

cabins

hull

Navigation

lighthouse

buoy

buoy

Taking a liner in and out of port can be difficult. Usually, a pilot who knows the port well takes control of the ship. Floating buoys show the pilot where the channels of deep water are. The flashing light on a lighthouse warns ships of dangerous rocks.

Navigation means finding the way. Once the ship is out on the open sea, the captain and crew on the bridge work out the ship's course using maps. They use radar to spot other ships, and sometimes satellite signals to check their position.

The engine room

Down in the hull are the ship's engines. Some ships have diesel engines, others have gas turbine engines. The engines turn the propeller, which drives the ship through the water. The rudder steers the ship.

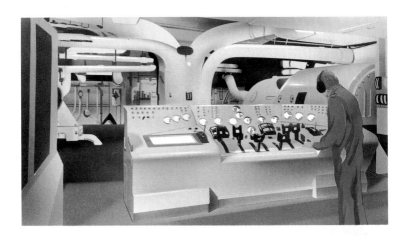

rudder

propeller

How a ship floats

The weight of a ship's hull pushes it down into the water. But the water tries to get back and pushes up against the hull. If the two pushes are equal, the ship floats. But if the ship is made too heavy, it will sink.

Marks on the ship's side, called the Plimsoll line, show how low in the water the ship can safely go.

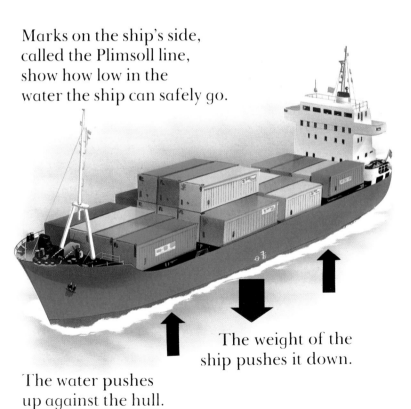

The weight of the ship pushes it down.

The water pushes up against the hull.

85

All kinds of ships

Ships come in different shapes and sizes.

A hydrofoil skims over the surface of the sea. It has underwater "wings" that lift it out of the water.

Hovercraft float on a cushion of air. Hidden fans blow air downward and lift the hovercraft off the water.

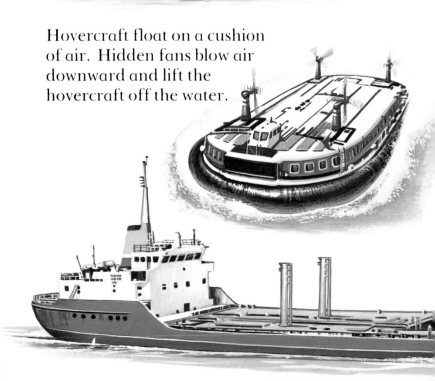

Paddle steamers travel up
and down rivers.
They are
driven by a
big wheel at
the stern.

Lifeboats rescue people at
sea. They are small, but
they are almost
unsinkable.

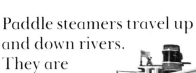

Fishing trawlers have a
winding engine at the
stern to haul in
their heavy nets.

FD 17

Supertankers carry oil
in huge tanks. They
are the biggest ships
in the world.

87

Canals

Canals are waterways built by people. When a canal runs through land that is on a slope, it must be built in a series of steps. To move up and down these steps, canal boats have to go through locks.

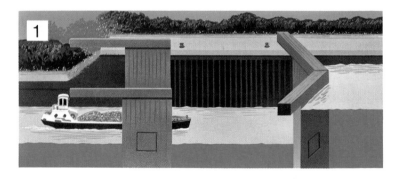

This canal boat is going up a step. Once the
boat is in the lock, the gates are closed.
Then water is slowly let into the lock. When
the water has risen to the correct level, the
gates open and the canal boat moves on.

Sailing ships

Sailing ships are powered by the wind pushing against the sails. Sailing ships like this one carried people and cargo over 100 years ago. But people stopped using big sailing ships when faster steamships were invented.

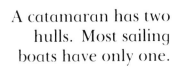

The junk is a Chinese sailing ship.

This racing yacht can go very fast. The big sail at the front is called a spinnaker.

A catamaran has two hulls. Most sailing boats have only one.

A submarine

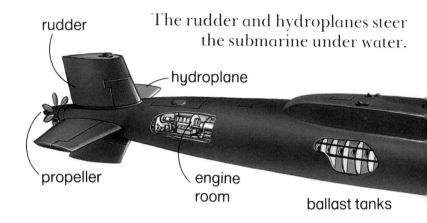

rudder

The rudder and hydroplanes steer the submarine under water.

hydroplane

propeller

engine room

ballast tanks

Submarines are ships that go under water. They can stay under water for weeks without coming to the surface. The commander controls the submarine from the control room. By raising the periscope, he can look around above the water.

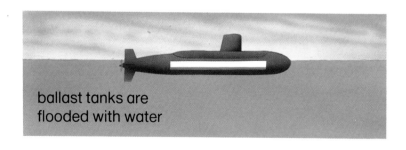

ballast tanks are flooded with water

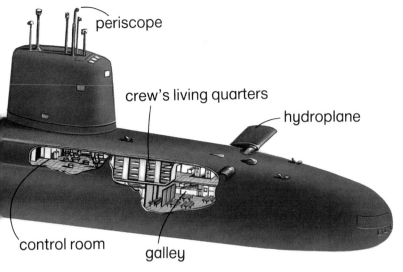

periscope

crew's living quarters

hydroplane

control room

galley

To dive, the submarine's ballast tanks are flooded with seawater. The submarine sinks. To come back up to the surface, air is blown into the ballast tanks, pushing out the water.

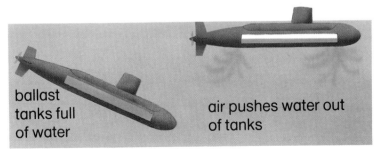

ballast tanks full of water

air pushes water out of tanks

Amazing facts

The first expedition to sail around the world was led by the explorer Ferdinand Magellan in 1519. The voyage took nearly three years and proved that the Earth is round, and not flat as many people had believed.

Over a hundred years ago, the fastest sailing ships were clipper ships. A clipper could cross the Atlantic in 12 days. The fastest crossing by a modern passenger liner is three and a half days.

The world's biggest ship is an oil tanker, *Hellas Foss*, of 611,838 tons. The largest passenger ship is the cruise liner *Norway*, which is over 1,000 feet long.

Famous shipwrecks include the English warship *Mary Rose* and the liner *Titanic*. The *Mary Rose* sank when it turned over in 1545, and the *Titanic* hit an iceberg in 1912.

Into

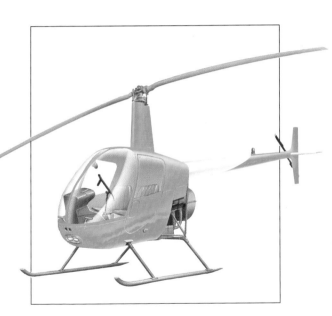

the air

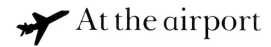 # At the airport

An airport needs lots of space. There are long runways, hangars for aircraft that need servicing and repairs, and terminal buildings where the passengers check in.

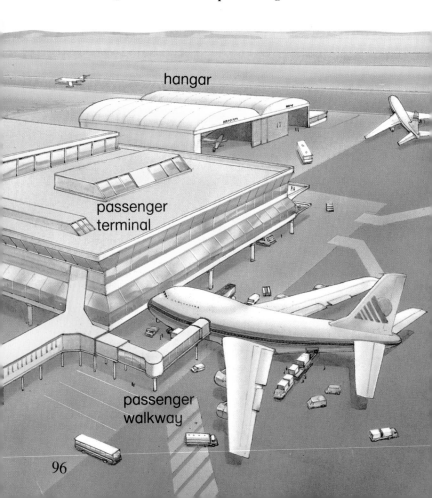

hangar

passenger
terminal

passenger
walkway

Before the passengers board their plane, it must be cleaned and refueled. Food is taken on board, and the baggage is stored in the hold. When everything is ready, the plane moves to the end of the runway to wait for permission to take off.

control tower

runway

✈ A jumbo jet

This Boeing 747 is the world's biggest passenger plane. It has room for about 400 passengers. Its four turbofan engines push it through the air at over 550 miles an hour. It has a wide body, called the fuselage, thin strong wings, and a big tailfin.

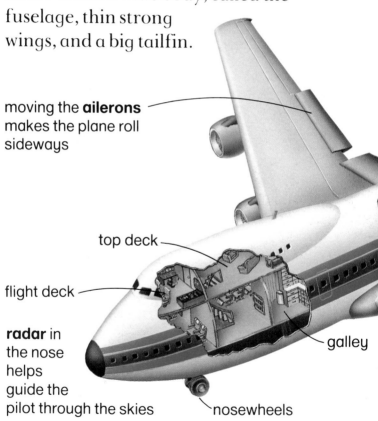

moving the **ailerons** makes the plane roll sideways

top deck

flight deck

radar in the nose helps guide the pilot through the skies

galley

nosewheels

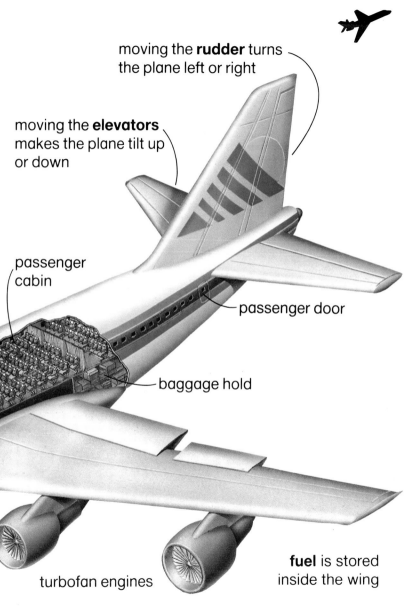

moving the **rudder** turns the plane left or right

moving the **elevators** makes the plane tilt up or down

passenger cabin

passenger door

baggage hold

fuel is stored inside the wing

turbofan engines

✈ Catching a plane

When passengers arrive at the airport, they check their baggage at the airline desk. If they are traveling abroad, they must then go through passport control.

loading the plane

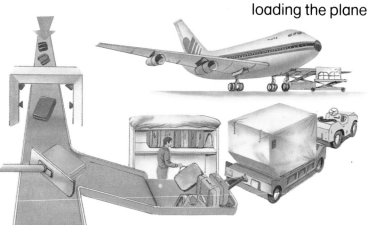

While passengers wait to board the plane, baggage handlers load their baggage into the plane's hold. During the flight, the cabin crew looks after the passengers. They serve drinks and meals. Once the plane has landed, the passengers collect their baggage.

unloading the plane

 # Permission to take off

The pilot waits for the controllers in the control tower to give him permission to take off. The controllers use radar to keep track of all the planes in the air or on the ground.

Computers on the flight deck help the pilot control the plane. They show him how high the plane is flying and how fast it is going. Even if the computers break down, the pilot can still fly the plane using instruments such as the altimeter and the artificial horizon.

altimeter

artificial horizon

✈ How a plane flies

As the engines drive the plane along the runway, air flows around the wings. The faster the plane goes, the faster the air flows.

The forward push that comes from the engines is called thrust.

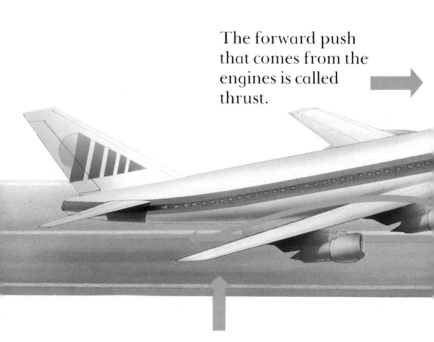

Air flowing over and under the curved wing creates lift.

The upward push is called lift.

The wings of a plane have a curved shape. When air flows over and under the wings, it creates an upward push beneath the plane. As the plane picks up speed, the upward push gets stronger. When it is strong enough, it lifts the plane off the ground.

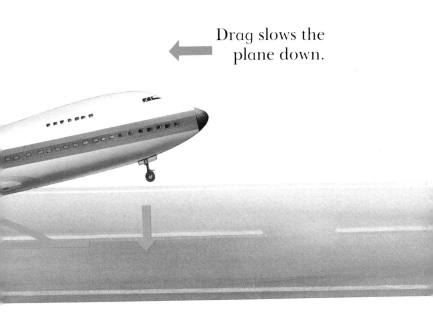

Drag slows the plane down.

The weight of the plane pulls it downward.

✈ All kinds of aircraft

Any flying machine is an aircraft. Aircraft can be huge or tiny. Some can fly faster than others, but each has a job to do.

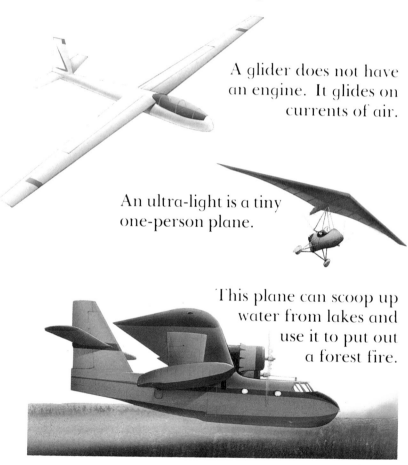

A glider does not have an engine. It glides on currents of air.

An ultra-light is a tiny one-person plane.

This plane can scoop up water from lakes and use it to put out a forest fire.

The Concorde is the only supersonic
airliner in the world.
"Supersonic" means that it can
fly faster than the
speed of sound.

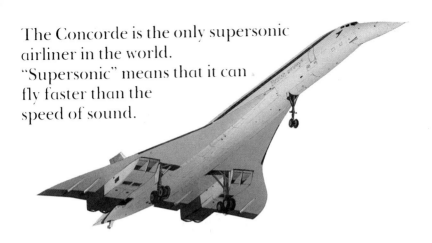

This small commuter jet
carries people on
business trips.

The Super Guppy looks like a flying whale.
It was built to carry the parts of other aircraft
and rockets.

 # Old planes

The first pilots were brave and skillful.
Their planes were small and slow, but they
made history in the air.

Orville and
Wilbur Wright flew the first real
airplane in 1903.

In 1909 Louis
Blériot was the first
person to fly across
the sea from France
to England.

In 1927 Charles Lindbergh was
the first pilot to fly across
the Atlantic Ocean alone.

✈ Military planes

Air forces and navies use special planes.
Some are very fast fighters and bombers.
Some, such as the Harrier jump jet, do not
need a long runway. They can land in a
field or on the deck of a ship.

Hornet

Mirage

Harrier

Helicopters

A helicopter has spinning rotor blades instead of wings. It can fly upward or downward or sideways and can even hover in midair.

To move the helicopter in all these different directions, the pilot changes the angle of the rotor blades using a joy stick and foot pedals.

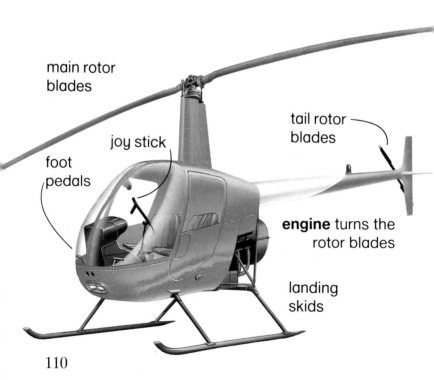

main rotor blades

tail rotor blades

joy stick

foot pedals

engine turns the rotor blades

landing skids

Helicopters are often used to rescue people
at sea. The pilot keeps the helicopter steady
while one of the crew members is lowered
on a line to help the person in the water.
Then both are winched up to safety.

111

Amazing facts

In 1933 Wiley Post was the first person to fly solo around the world. His journey was 15,596 miles long and took him 7 days, 18 hours, and 49 minutes.

In 1986 a plane flew nonstop around the world without refueling. Two pilots were squashed inside the small cabin for 9 days, 3 minutes, and 44 seconds.

The world's heaviest aircraft is the Russian An-225 *Dream*. It weighs 519 tons.

The fastest aircraft of all time was the American X-15A-2, a rocket plane that reached 4,520 miles an hour in 1967.

The Harrier jump jet is a V/STOL plane. This means that it can fly straight up or down. The letters V/STOL stand for "vertical and short takeoff and landing."

The

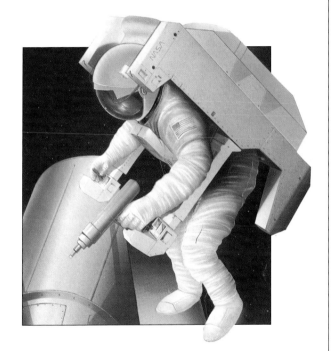

Space Age

Lift-off

It takes five engines, burning 22 tons of fuel a second, to lift the space shuttle off the launch pad. The shuttle can carry up to seven astronauts into space. It can also carry satellites and a laboratory in its large payload bay.

main fuel tank

payload bay

booster rockets give extra power during launch

About two minutes after lift-off, the two booster rockets fall away from the shuttle and parachute into the sea.

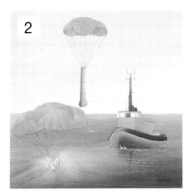
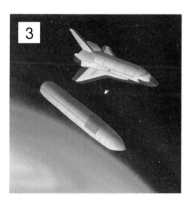

A few minutes later, the main fuel tank also falls away. Once its mission is over, the shuttle returns to Earth and lands on a runway like an airplane.

# On board the shuttle

The living area and the flight deck are in the nose of the shuttle. In the middle is the payload bay. Once the shuttle is out in space, the doors of the payload bay can open. On this mission the shuttle is carrying a telescope and a spacelab.

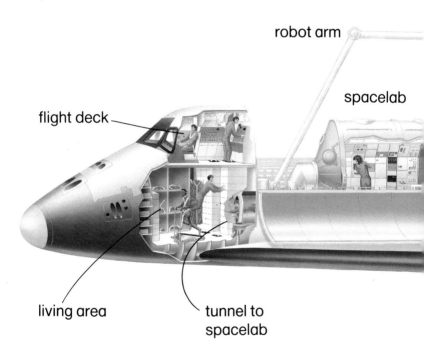

robot arm

spacelab

flight deck

living area

tunnel to spacelab

The astronauts carry out scientific experiments in the lab. One of the astronauts is working out in the payload bay. He is attached to a robot arm so he doesn't float away.

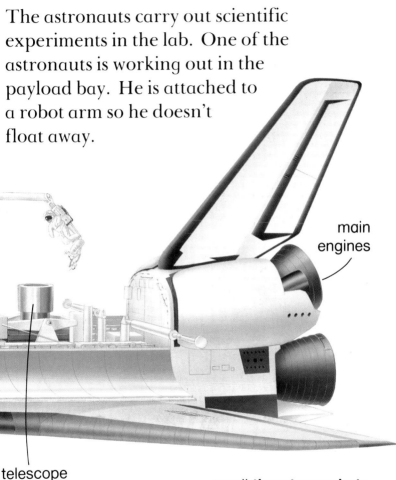

main engines

telescope

small **thruster rockets** move the shuttle while it is in space

Life in Space

In space there is no gravity. So unless they are strapped down, the astronauts float around inside the shuttle. They even have to strap themselves onto the exercise machine and into their sleeping bags.

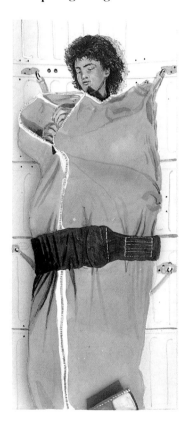

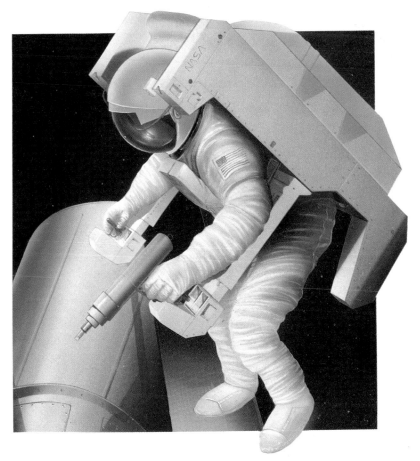

Because there is no air in
space, astronauts must wear a spacesuit
when they are working outside the shuttle.
This astronaut is also wearing an MMU —
a Man Maneuvering Unit. By firing jets in
the MMU, the astronaut can move around.

Amazing facts

The Space Age began in 1957, when the USSR launched the first artificial satellite. It was called *Sputnik I*.

The world's first human space traveler was Yuri Gagarin of the USSR. He traveled once around the Earth in 1961.

The first people to land on the Moon were the American astronauts Neil Armstrong and Edwin Aldrin. They landed in the *Apollo 11* spacecraft on July 20, 1969.

In 1977 the United States launched the *Voyager 2* robot spacecraft on a voyage of exploration. It sent back television pictures of four planets – Jupiter, Saturn, Uranus, and Neptune – and is still traveling out in space.

INDEX

The editor would like to thank Trans World Airlines Inc. and the many other companies and individuals who assisted in the preparation of this book.